THE INDIAN DIASPORA

AN EXPLORATION OF THE INDIAN COMMUNITY LIVING ABROAD AND ITS CULTURE

DR. JAGADEESH PILLAI

|| Dedicated to all wisdom seekers around the World ||

ॐ

Contents

Contents

Prayer

**"Om Bhadram Karnebhih Shrunuyaama
DevaahBhadram Pashyemaakshabhiryajatraah
SthirairangaistushtuvaamsastanoobhihVyashema
Devahitam YadaayuhSwasti Na Indro
VridhashravaahSwasti Nah Pooshaa
VishwavedaahSwasti Nastaarkshyo ArishtanemihSwasti
No Brihaspatir DadhaatuOm Shantih, Shantih, Shantih"**

The literal meaning of this mantra is: OM. O Gods! Let us
hear auspicious words from our ears. O reverent Gods! Let
us behold propitious visions from our eyes, let our organs
and body be stable, healthy, and strong. Let us do that
which is pleasing to the gods in the life span allotted to us.
May Indra, inscribed in the scriptures, bring us fortune!
May Pushan, the knower of the world, grant us prosperity!
May Trakshya, who vanquishes enemies, bestow us with
blessings! May Brihaspati bring us success!
OM Peace, Peace, Peace.

About The Author

Dr. Jagadeesh Pillai is a renowned Guinness World Record holder, writer, and researcher hailing from Varanasi, also known as the abode of Lord Shiva. With a Ph.D. in Vedic Science and a range of creative ideas and achievements, he is a true polymath. He is the author of more than 100 books including Research Publications. Although his roots can be traced back to Kerala, the people of Varanasi hold him in high regard and affectionately consider him one of their own.

In 1998, Dr. Pillai was offered a job at Banaras Hindu University, but he left the position after only two months to pursue greater goals in life. He believed that in order to study Indian scriptures and engage in other creative endeavours, he needed to retire from the daily grind of working solely for money at a young age.

He started an export business from scratch, using the knowledge he had gained from a previous job in the industry. His intelligence and unique approach to business led to great success in a short period of time, earning him more in just a decade and a half than he would have in a lifetime working in a government job. Upon the passing of Dr. APJ Abdul Kalam, Dr. Pillai decided to leave the business and dedicate himself to reading, studying, researching, and experimenting.

During his tenure in the export business, Dr. Pillai traveled to over 16 countries, gaining valuable insight and experiencing the world and life in detail.

Dr. Pillai has achieved four Guinness World Records in the following subjects:

"Script to Screen" - In this record, Dr. Pillai produced and directed an animation film within the shortest time possible, breaking the previous record set by Canadians. He has also received numerous national and international awards and recognitions for this achievement.

Longest Line of Postcards - For this record, Dr. Pillai created a line of 16,300 postcards on the occasion of the 163rd anniversary of Indian Postal Day. The event also included a questionnaire about the Indian flag.

Largest Poster Awareness Campaign - Dr. Pillai designed an awareness campaign on the subject of "Beti Bachao - Beti Padhao" (Save the Girl Child - Educate the Girl Child) to achieve this record.

Largest Envelope - In tribute to the Indian Prime Minister's "Make in India" initiative, Dr. Pillai created a 4000 square meter envelope using waste paper to achieve this record.

Attempted - **70000 Candles on a 210 kg Cake** - To celebrate the 70th Indian Independence Day, Dr. Pillai attempted to light 70,000 candles on a 210 kg cake, which was recorded in World Records India.

Attempted - **Documentary on Dhamek Stupa of Sarnath in 17 Languages** - Dr. Pillai attempted to create a documentary on the Dhamek Stupa of Sarnath, dubbing it in 17 different languages. The result of this attempt is currently awaiting confirmation from the Guinness World Records.

Dr. Pillai is skilled in teaching the Bhagavad Gita, a Hindu scripture, and is popular among young people. He has helped many young people improve their lives through his motivational teachings.

In addition to teaching, he has composed and sung numerous Sanskrit Bhajans and patriotic songs.

He has also written and directed several short films and documentaries for awareness campaigns, and has volunteered with the police in both UP and Kerala to spread awareness about various issues through videos and photography.

Incredibly, he has produced and directed over 100 documentaries about the city of Varanasi, all on his own.

He has also helped and guided more than 25 boys and girls to achieve world records through creative and innovative methods. He is a multifaceted person who uses his intellect and the blessings given to him by God to excel in various areas. He is both a teacher and a student, always learning and teaching, and is able to master any subject he comes across.

He is a selfless social activist and motivational speaker who has overcome struggles and failures to become a successful and enthusiastic individual with a rich life experience.

In addition to his work with the Bhagavad Gita, he is also an efficient Tarot card reader, Astro-Vastu consultant, and a talented singer and composer. He has sung the entire Ram Charita Manas and Bhagavad Gita in his own compositions, and has sung the phrase "Lokah Samastha Sukhino Bhavantu" in 50 different languages. He is currently working on a detailed and scientific study of Vedas, Upanishads, Puranas, and the Bhagavad Gita. He has also composed and sung the Hanuman Chalisa and Gayatri Mantra in 108 and 1008 different compositions, respectively.

Awards - Four Times Guinness World Records, Winner of Mahatma Gandhi Vishwa Shanti Puraskar, Mahatma Gandhi Global Peace Ambassador, Kashi Ratna Award, Dr. APJ Abdul Kalam Motivational Person of the Year 2017, Mother Teresa Award, Indira Gandhi Priyadarshini Award, Bharat Vikas Ratna Award, Udyog Ratna Award, Vigyan Prasar Award, Poorvanchal Ratn Samman.

PREFACE

The Indian Diaspora is a global phenomenon that has had a significant impact on Indian culture, society, and the countries where they have settled. The Indian community abroad has made substantial contributions to the cultural, social, and economic development of the countries where they have settled, as well as to the preservation of their cultural identity and heritage. This book, titled "The Indian Diaspora: An Exploration of The Indian Community Living Abroad and its Culture," provides a comprehensive examination of the Indian Diaspora, exploring its cultural, social, and economic contributions, as well as its political and historical significance.

This book is intended to provide a comprehensive understanding of the Indian Diaspora, and to shed light on the diverse experiences of the Indian community abroad. Through detailed research and analysis, this book provides an in-depth examination of the various aspects of the Indian Diaspora, including its impact on the host countries, its economic contributions, its political participation, and its efforts to preserve its cultural identity and heritage.

The authors of this book are experts in the field of Indian Diaspora studies, and have extensively researched and written about the subject. They bring a wealth of knowledge and experience to the table, and provide a nuanced understanding of the Indian Diaspora that is both insightful and informative.

This book is a must-read for anyone who is interested in

learning about the Indian Diaspora and its impact on the world. Whether you are a student of history, culture, or economics, or simply someone who is interested in learning more about this fascinating community, this book is sure to provide you with a wealth of information and understanding. So, come join us on this journey of exploration and discovery as we delve into the world of the Indian Diaspora and its impact on Indian culture and society.

I

Introduction: Understanding the Indian Diaspora

The Indian diaspora refers to the widespread community of people of Indian origin who have settled in countries across the world. The Indian diaspora has a rich history and a unique cultural identity that has been shaped by centuries of migration, adaptation, and preservation. It is a diverse community, with members originating from different parts of India and speaking different languages, practicing different religions, and having distinct regional customs and traditions.

The Indian diaspora can be traced back to ancient times when merchants and traders traveled to far-off lands in search of new markets and opportunities. During the colonial era, many Indians were forced to migrate to other countries as indentured laborers, while others moved to pursue education and work opportunities. In the modern era, Indian migration has been driven by a variety of factors, including economic growth, political instability, and the search for a better life for themselves and their families.

Despite the differences in their backgrounds and experiences, members of the Indian diaspora are united by a shared cultural heritage and a strong sense of identity. They have maintained and passed down their traditions, values, and beliefs from generation to generation, preserving their cultural heritage even as they have adapted to their new environments.

The Indian diaspora has also made significant contributions to their adopted countries, enriching local cultures and communities with their unique perspectives, customs, and traditions. They have also established vibrant communities, complete with religious and cultural organizations, festivals, and social events, which serve as a way to connect with each other and their roots.

In this book, we will explore the Indian diaspora in-depth, examining its history, cultural identity, and the experiences of its members. Through the stories of individual diaspora members, we will gain a better understanding of what it means to be part of this vibrant and diverse community, and how it has impacted the world in which it exists. We will delve into the cultural traditions, customs, and beliefs of the Indian diaspora, as well as the challenges and opportunities that they have faced and created in their adopted countries.

In the following chapters, we will explore the Indian diaspora in various regions of the world, including North America, Europe, Africa, and Asia. We will also examine the role of the Indian diaspora in politics, business, and the arts, and how they are shaping the world in which they live. Whether you are a member of the Indian diaspora, an admirer of Indian culture, or simply someone interested in learning about the experiences of this fascinating community, this book offers a comprehensive and insightful look at the Indian diaspora and its place in the world today.

"The Indian Diaspora represents a bridge between India and the world, connecting cultures and fostering mutual understanding."

৪৩

II

The Historical Context of the Indian Diaspora

The Indian diaspora has a long and rich history that dates back several centuries. Over the centuries, people of Indian origin have migrated to various parts of the world in search of new opportunities, better living conditions, and to escape political or economic unrest. The historical context of the Indian diaspora is marked by a complex interplay of various political, economic, and cultural factors that have shaped the experiences of its members.

One of the earliest examples of Indian migration can be traced back to ancient times when Indian merchants and traders traveled to far-off lands in search of new markets. These early travelers established trade routes and brought Indian goods, ideas, and culture to the lands they visited. They also played a key role in spreading Buddhism, which had a profound impact on the cultures and religions of many Asian countries.

The colonial era had a significant impact on the Indian diaspora. During this period, many Indians were forced to migrate as indentured laborers to countries such as South Africa, the Caribbean, and Southeast Asia to work on sugar plantations and other labor-intensive industries. The harsh working conditions and discriminatory policies they faced in their adopted countries often led to a loss of cultural identity and a disconnection from their roots.

In the 20th century, the Indian diaspora experienced another wave of migration, driven by a variety of factors such as political instability, economic growth, and the search for better living conditions. Indian professionals, entrepreneurs, and students have migrated to countries such as the United States, Canada, the United Kingdom, and Australia in search of better work opportunities and education.

The experiences of the Indian diaspora have been shaped not only by the historical context in which they lived but also by the policies and attitudes of their adopted countries. In many cases, Indian migrants faced discrimination and prejudice, and were often subjected to racial and cultural stereotypes. Despite these challenges, the Indian diaspora has persevered, maintaining their cultural heritage and creating vibrant communities in their adopted countries.

The Indian diaspora has also played a significant role in shaping the political, economic, and cultural landscapes of their adopted countries. Indian migrants have established businesses, organizations, and cultural institutions that have enriched local communities and helped to promote Indian culture abroad. They have also been active in politics, advocating for the rights of migrant communities and working to promote cultural exchange and understanding.

"The Indian community abroad has made
significant contributions to the cultural,
social, and economic development of the
countries where they have settled."

౸

III

The Indian Diaspora in Southeast Asia

The Indian diaspora has had a profound impact on Southeast Asian countries, particularly Indonesia, Malaysia, and Singapore. The Indian community has made a significant contribution to the region's cultural, economic, and political landscapes and has played a key role in shaping its history.

The Indian diaspora in Southeast Asia dates back to ancient times when Indian merchants and traders traveled to the region in search of new markets and trade opportunities. Over time, the Indian community established itself as a vibrant and integral part of Southeast Asian society, playing a key role in the region's cultural, economic, and political development.

One of the most significant contributions of the Indian diaspora in Southeast Asia was the spread of Hinduism and Buddhism, which had a profound impact on the region's cultures and religions. The Indian community also introduced its cuisine, music, and dance to Southeast Asia, which has since become an integral part of the region's cultural heritage.

The Indian diaspora has also played a key role in the region's economic development, particularly in the fields of trade, commerce, and industry. Indian migrants established businesses and trade networks that helped to connect Southeast Asia to the rest of the world. They also played a key role in the region's agriculture, particularly in the cultivation of spices and other cash crops.

The Indian diaspora has also been active in politics, advocating for the rights of migrant communities and working to promote cultural exchange and understanding. In many cases, Indian migrants have faced discrimination and prejudice, and have been subjected to racial and cultural stereotypes. Despite these challenges, the Indian diaspora has persevered, maintaining their cultural heritage and creating vibrant communities in their adopted countries.

In the following chapters, we will examine the Indian diaspora in Southeast Asia in greater detail, exploring its roots, evolution, and impact on the region. By understanding the experiences and challenges faced by the Indian diaspora in Southeast Asia, we can gain a deeper appreciation for the unique cultural heritage they have created and preserved.

The Indian diaspora in Southeast Asia is an integral part of the region's cultural, economic, and political heritage. The Indian community has made a significant contribution to the region's development and has played a key role in shaping its history. Through their perseverance and determination, the Indian diaspora has maintained its cultural heritage and created vibrant communities in their adopted countries, despite the challenges they have faced.

"The Indian Diaspora serves as a testament
to the resilience and determination of the
Indian people, and their ability to succeed
and thrive in new and challenging
environments."

☙

IV

The Indian Diaspora in the Caribbean

The Indian diaspora has had a profound impact on the Caribbean region, particularly in countries like Guyana, Trinidad and Tobago, and Jamaica. The Indian community has made a significant contribution to the region's cultural, economic, and political landscapes and has played a key role in shaping its history.

The Indian diaspora in the Caribbean dates back to the late 19th century, when Indian indentured laborers were brought to the region to work on sugar plantations. Over time, the Indian community established itself as a vibrant and integral part of Caribbean society, playing a key role in the region's cultural, economic, and political development.

One of the most significant contributions of the Indian

diaspora in the Caribbean was the preservation and transmission of their cultural heritage. Despite facing discrimination and prejudice, the Indian community has maintained its traditions, values, and language, creating a unique cultural identity in their adopted countries. This has had a profound impact on the region's cultural landscape, enriching its diversity and heritage.

The Indian diaspora has also played a key role in the region's economic development, particularly in the fields of trade, commerce, and industry. Indian migrants established businesses and trade networks that helped to connect the Caribbean to the rest of the world. They also played a key role in the region's agriculture, particularly in the cultivation of spices and other cash crops.

The Indian diaspora has also been active in politics, advocating for the rights of migrant communities and working to promote cultural exchange and understanding. In many cases, Indian migrants have faced discrimination and prejudice, and have been subjected to racial and cultural stereotypes. Despite these challenges, the Indian diaspora has persevered, maintaining their cultural heritage and creating vibrant communities in their adopted countries.

In the following chapters, we will examine the Indian diaspora in the Caribbean in greater detail, exploring its roots, evolution, and impact on the region. By understanding the experiences and challenges faced by the Indian diaspora in the Caribbean, we can gain a deeper appreciation for the unique cultural heritage they have created and preserved.

The Indian diaspora in the Caribbean is an integral part of the region's cultural, economic, and political heritage. The Indian community has made a significant contribution to the region's development and has played a key role in shaping its history. Through their perseverance and determination, the Indian diaspora has maintained its cultural heritage and created vibrant communities in their adopted countries, despite the challenges they have faced.

*"The preservation of cultural identity and
heritage is a central part of the Indian
Diaspora experience, as they strive to
maintain their cultural traditions and values
in a foreign land."*

ॐ

V

The Indian Diaspora in the Middle East

The Indian diaspora in the Middle East has a long and rich history that dates back several centuries. Over the years, the Indian community has established itself as an integral part of the social, cultural, and economic fabric of the region, playing a significant role in shaping its development.

The first Indian migrants to the Middle East were traders, who established themselves in the region as early as the 7th century. Over time, the Indian community grew and diversified, with many Indian workers and professionals settling in the region to work in a range of industries, including construction, finance, and healthcare.

The Indian diaspora in the Middle East has made a significant contribution to the region's cultural landscape, preserving and transmitting its cultural heritage. Despite facing challenges and discrimination, the Indian community has maintained its traditions, values, and language, creating a unique cultural identity in its adopted countries. This has had a profound impact on the region's cultural heritage, enriching its diversity and preserving its rich history.

The Indian diaspora has also played a key role in the region's economic development, particularly in the fields of trade, commerce, and industry. Indian migrants have established businesses and trade networks that have helped to connect the Middle East to the rest of the world. They have also played a key role in the region's service sector, particularly in the fields of healthcare, education, and finance.

In addition to its cultural and economic contributions, the Indian diaspora has also been active in politics, advocating for the rights of migrant communities and working to promote cultural exchange and understanding. Despite the challenges they have faced, Indian migrants have persevered, maintaining their cultural heritage and creating vibrant communities in their adopted countries.

In the following chapters, we will examine the Indian diaspora in the Middle East in greater detail, exploring its roots, evolution, and impact on the region. By understanding the experiences and challenges faced by the Indian diaspora in the Middle East, we can gain a deeper appreciation for the unique cultural heritage they have created and preserved.

The Indian diaspora in the Middle East is an integral part of the region's cultural, economic, and political heritage. The Indian community has made a significant contribution to the region's development and has played a key role in shaping its history. Through their perseverance and determination, the Indian diaspora has maintained its cultural heritage and created vibrant communities in their adopted countries, despite the challenges they have faced.

"The Indian Diaspora has made an indelible impact on the global community, and its contributions to the world of art, literature, music, and science are immeasurable."

৪৩

VI

The Indian Diaspora in Africa

The Indian diaspora in Africa is a vibrant and dynamic community that has a long and rich history dating back several centuries. Over the years, Indian migrants have established themselves as an integral part of the social, cultural, and economic fabric of the continent, playing a significant role in shaping its development.

The first Indian migrants to Africa arrived on the continent as traders and merchants, establishing themselves in cities such as Mombasa, Durban, and Cape Town. Over time, the Indian community grew and diversified, with many Indian workers and professionals settling in the region to work in a range of industries, including agriculture, finance, and healthcare.

The Indian diaspora in Africa has made a significant contribution to the continent's cultural landscape, preserving and transmitting its cultural heritage. Despite facing challenges and discrimination, the Indian community has maintained its traditions, values, and language, creating a unique cultural identity in its adopted countries. This has had a profound impact on the continent's cultural heritage, enriching its diversity and preserving its rich history.

The Indian diaspora has also played a key role in the continent's economic development, particularly in the fields of trade, commerce, and industry. Indian migrants have established businesses and trade networks that have helped to connect Africa to the rest of the world. They have also played a key role in the continent's service sector, particularly in the fields of healthcare, education, and finance.

In addition to its cultural and economic contributions, the Indian diaspora has also been active in politics, advocating for the rights of migrant communities and working to promote cultural exchange and understanding. Despite the challenges they have faced, Indian migrants have persevered, maintaining their cultural heritage and creating vibrant communities in their adopted countries.

In the following chapters, we will examine the Indian diaspora in Africa in greater detail, exploring its roots, evolution, and impact on the continent. By understanding the experiences and challenges faced by the Indian diaspora in Africa, we can gain a deeper appreciation for the unique cultural heritage they have created and preserved.

The Indian diaspora in Africa is an integral part of the continent's cultural, economic, and political heritage. The Indian community has made a significant contribution to the continent's development and has played a key role in shaping its history. Through their perseverance and determination, the Indian diaspora has maintained its cultural heritage and created vibrant communities in their adopted countries, despite the challenges they have faced.

"The Indian Diaspora represents a rich
tapestry of cultures, languages, and
traditions, showcasing the diversity and
strength of the Indian people."

ॐ

VII

The Indian Diaspora in Europe

The Indian diaspora in Europe is a diverse and dynamic community that has a long and rich history, dating back several centuries. Over the years, Indian migrants have established themselves as an integral part of the social, cultural, and economic fabric of the region, playing a significant role in shaping its development.

The first Indian migrants to Europe arrived as traders, merchants, and students. Over time, the Indian community grew and diversified, with many Indian workers and professionals settling in the region to work in a range of industries, including technology, finance, and healthcare. Today, the Indian diaspora in Europe is a vibrant and thriving community, numbering in the millions and spread across the continent.

The Indian diaspora in Europe has made a significant

contribution to the region's cultural landscape, preserving and transmitting its cultural heritage. Despite facing challenges and discrimination, the Indian community has maintained its traditions, values, and language, creating a unique cultural identity in its adopted countries. This has had a profound impact on the region's cultural heritage, enriching its diversity and preserving its rich history.

The Indian diaspora has also played a key role in the region's economic development, particularly in the fields of technology and finance. Indian migrants have established businesses and trade networks that have helped to connect Europe to the rest of the world. They have also played a key role in the region's service sector, particularly in the fields of healthcare, education, and finance.

In addition to its cultural and economic contributions, the Indian diaspora has also been active in politics, advocating for the rights of migrant communities and working to promote cultural exchange and understanding. Despite the challenges they have faced, Indian migrants have persevered, maintaining their cultural heritage and creating vibrant communities in their adopted countries.

In the following chapters, we will examine the Indian diaspora in Europe in greater detail, exploring its roots, evolution, and impact on the region. By understanding the experiences and challenges faced by the Indian diaspora in Europe, we can gain a deeper appreciation for the unique cultural heritage they have created and preserved.

The Indian diaspora in Europe is an integral part of the region's cultural, economic, and political heritage. The

Indian community has made a significant contribution to the region's development and has played a key role in shaping its history. Through their perseverance and determination, the Indian diaspora has maintained its cultural heritage and created vibrant communities in their adopted countries, despite the challenges they have faced.

"The Indian Diaspora has been instrumental
in the growth and development of the
economies of the countries where they have
settled, creating jobs and fostering
innovation."

ಧ

VIII

The Indian diaspora in North America

The Indian diaspora in North America is a large and dynamic community, comprising millions of individuals from various regions of India who have made their homes in the United States and Canada. The community has a rich and diverse history, with the first Indian migrants arriving in North America in the late 19th and early 20th centuries.

Initially, Indian migrants to North America consisted mainly of laborers, merchants, and students. Over time, the community grew and diversified, with Indian professionals and entrepreneurs settling in the region and making significant contributions to the fields of technology, finance, and healthcare. Today, the Indian diaspora in North America is a thriving and vibrant community, with a rich cultural heritage and a significant impact on the region's social, cultural, and economic landscape.

The Indian diaspora in North America has played a critical role in preserving and transmitting the cultural heritage of India, creating a unique cultural identity in its adopted countries. Despite facing challenges and discrimination, the Indian community has maintained its traditions, values, and language, enriching the region's cultural landscape and preserving its rich history.

In addition to its cultural contributions, the Indian diaspora in North America has made a significant impact on the region's economy, particularly in the fields of technology and finance. Indian migrants have established businesses and trade networks that have helped to connect North America to the rest of the world, playing a key role in the region's economic growth and development.

The Indian diaspora in North America has also been active in politics, advocating for the rights of migrant communities and working to promote cultural exchange and understanding. Despite the challenges they have faced, Indian migrants have persevered, maintaining their cultural heritage and creating vibrant communities in their adopted countries.

In the following chapters, we will examine the Indian diaspora in North America in greater detail, exploring its roots, evolution, and impact on the region. By understanding the experiences and challenges faced by the Indian diaspora in North America, we can gain a deeper appreciation for the unique cultural heritage they have created and preserved.

The Indian diaspora in North America is an integral part of the region's cultural, economic, and political heritage. The Indian community has made a significant contribution to the region's development and has played a key role in shaping its history. Through their perseverance and determination, the Indian diaspora has maintained its cultural heritage and created vibrant communities in their adopted countries, despite the challenges they have faced.

"The Indian Diaspora's political
participation and activism have helped shape
the policies and governance of the countries
where they have settled, making their voices
heard and ensuring their rights and interests
are protected."

૪૭

IX

The Indian Diaspora in Australia and New Zealand

The Indian diaspora in Australia and New Zealand is a vibrant and dynamic community, comprised of individuals from various regions of India who have made their homes in these countries. The Indian community has a rich history in both countries, with the first migrants arriving in Australia in the mid-19th century and in New Zealand in the late 19th century.

In Australia, the Indian diaspora initially consisted of laborers, merchants, and students. Over time, the community grew and diversified, with Indian professionals and entrepreneurs settling in the country and making significant contributions to its social, cultural, and economic landscape. Today, the Indian diaspora in Australia is a thriving and vibrant community, with a rich cultural heritage and a significant impact on the country's social and cultural landscape.

In New Zealand, the Indian diaspora has played a similar role, with migrants establishing themselves as business owners and professionals, contributing to the country's economic growth and development. The Indian community has also been active in preserving its cultural heritage and traditions, enriching New Zealand's cultural landscape and playing a key role in promoting cultural exchange and understanding.

Despite facing challenges and discrimination, the Indian diaspora in Australia and New Zealand has maintained its cultural heritage and traditions, creating vibrant communities that preserve the rich cultural heritage of India. Indian migrants have established religious and cultural organizations, festivals, and events, connecting the community to its roots and preserving its cultural heritage for future generations.

In addition to its cultural contributions, the Indian diaspora in Australia and New Zealand has made a significant impact on the region's economy, particularly in the fields of trade, tourism, and technology. Indian businesses have established trade networks and partnerships, connecting these countries to the rest of the world and playing a key role in their economic growth and development.

The Indian diaspora in Australia and New Zealand has also

been active in politics, advocating for the rights of migrant communities and working to promote cultural exchange and understanding. Despite the challenges they have faced, Indian migrants have persevered, maintaining their cultural heritage and creating vibrant communities in their adopted countries.

In the following chapters, we will examine the Indian diaspora in Australia and New Zealand in greater detail, exploring its roots, evolution, and impact on these countries. By understanding the experiences and challenges faced by the Indian diaspora in Australia and New Zealand, we can gain a deeper appreciation for the unique cultural heritage they have created and preserved.

The Indian diaspora in Australia and New Zealand is an integral part of these countries' cultural, economic, and political heritage. The Indian community has made a significant contribution to their development and has played a key role in shaping their history. Through their perseverance and determination, the Indian diaspora has maintained its cultural heritage and created vibrant communities in their adopted countries, despite the challenges they have faced.

"The Indian Diaspora has brought new and innovative ideas to the countries where they have settled, enriching and transforming local cultures and communities."

৪৩

X

The Indian Diaspora and its impact on Indian Culture and Society

The Indian Diaspora is the collective term used to describe the large number of people of Indian descent who have settled in different parts of the world. These individuals have left their homes in India in search of better economic and educational opportunities, and have formed thriving communities in various countries across the globe. The impact of the Indian Diaspora on Indian culture and society has been significant and far-reaching, and is worth exploring in greater detail.

One of the most obvious ways in which the Indian Diaspora has impacted Indian culture and society is through the spread of Indian traditions and values. The Indian community abroad has worked hard to preserve their cultural heritage, and has successfully passed on their traditions to the next generation. This has resulted in the preservation and promotion of Indian culture in different parts of the world. For example, the Hindu festivals of Diwali and Holi are now celebrated not just in India, but also in countries with a significant Indian population, such as the United Kingdom, the United States, and South Africa.

The Indian Diaspora has also had a profound impact on the Indian economy. Indian nationals working abroad send a large amount of money back to India in the form of remittances. These remittances play a crucial role in supporting the families of the Indian workers, and also contribute to the development of the Indian economy as a whole. In fact, India is one of the largest recipients of remittances in the world, with a significant portion of these funds coming from the Indian Diaspora.

The Indian Diaspora has also had a positive impact on Indian society through the sharing of knowledge and skills. Many of the Indians living abroad have gained expertise in various fields, such as medicine, engineering, and technology. Upon their return to India, they bring with them new ideas and innovative solutions that can benefit Indian society. For example, Indian doctors who have trained and worked in the United States often return to India with a wealth of knowledge and expertise that they use to provide better healthcare services to their patients.

The Indian Diaspora has had a significant impact on Indian culture and society. Through their efforts to preserve their cultural heritage, their contribution to the Indian economy, and their sharing of knowledge and skills, the Indian community abroad has helped shape the course of Indian history and has left a lasting impact on the country. The Indian Diaspora is an important aspect of the Indian community, and its influence on Indian culture and society is a topic that deserves further exploration and examination.

"The Indian Diaspora's hard work and
determination have allowed them to achieve
great success in their adopted countries, and
their contributions serve as an inspiration to
others."

৩

XI

The Indian Diaspora and its Impact on the Host Countries

The Indian Diaspora has had a profound impact on the countries that have welcomed Indian immigrants. The presence of the Indian community abroad has enriched the cultural landscape of these countries and has contributed to their economic and social development. In this chapter, we will explore the ways in which the Indian Diaspora has impacted the host countries and the various challenges that they have faced along the way.

One of the most notable ways in which the Indian Diaspora has impacted host countries is through the introduction of Indian culture. The Indian community abroad has worked hard to preserve their cultural heritage, and this has resulted in the spread of Indian traditions and values to the countries where they have settled. For example, the Hindu festivals of Diwali and Holi are now celebrated in many parts of the world, and have become an integral part of the cultural landscape in countries with a significant Indian population.

The Indian Diaspora has also had a positive impact on the economies of host countries. Many of the Indian immigrants have established businesses and have made significant contributions to the local economy. Indian-owned businesses are known for their entrepreneurial spirit and hard work, and have created jobs and boosted economic growth in the countries where they have settled. Additionally, the remittances that Indian workers send back to their families in India have also had a positive impact on the economies of the host countries, as these funds are often used to purchase goods and services.

However, the Indian Diaspora has also faced various challenges in the countries where they have settled. One of the biggest challenges that they have faced is discrimination and prejudice. Despite their contributions to the local economy and society, many Indian immigrants have faced racism and xenophobia in the countries where they have settled. This has resulted in feelings of isolation and marginalization for the Indian community abroad.

The Indian Diaspora has had a significant impact on the countries where they have settled. Through their contributions to the local economy, the introduction of Indian culture, and their hard work and entrepreneurial spirit, the Indian community abroad has made a lasting impact on the countries that have welcomed them. Despite the challenges that they have faced, the Indian Diaspora continues to play a vital role in the development of the countries where they have settled, and their presence has enriched the cultural landscape of these countries.

XII

The Indian Diaspora and its Economic Contributions

The Indian Diaspora has made a significant contribution to the economies of the countries where they have settled. Through their hard work, entrepreneurial spirit, and commitment to financial success, the Indian community abroad has played a vital role in the growth and development of the local economy. In this chapter, we will explore the ways in which the Indian Diaspora has made an impact on the economy and the various challenges that they have faced along the way.

One of the most notable ways in which the Indian Diaspora has contributed to the local economy is through their establishment of businesses. Indian immigrants have a long history of entrepreneurship, and have established a wide range of businesses in the countries where they have settled. These businesses range from small corner stores to large corporations, and have created jobs and boosted economic growth in the local community. Additionally, the Indian community abroad is known for their work ethic and dedication to success, which has made them valuable contributors to the local economy.

The Indian Diaspora has also made a significant contribution to the economy through the remittances that they send back to India. Many of the Indians living abroad send a portion of their income back to their families in India, and these remittances play a crucial role in supporting the families of the Indian workers. Additionally, these remittances contribute to the development of the Indian economy as a whole, as they are often used to purchase goods and services.

However, the Indian Diaspora has also faced various challenges in the countries where they have settled, particularly with regards to their economic success. One of the biggest challenges that they have faced is discrimination and prejudice in the workplace. Despite their contributions to the local economy and their hard work, many Indian immigrants have faced racism and xenophobia in the workplace, which has made it difficult for them to achieve financial success.

The Indian Diaspora has made a significant impact on the economies of the countries where they have settled. Through their establishment of businesses, their dedication to financial success, and their remittances back to India, the Indian community abroad has played a vital role in the growth and development of the local economy. Despite the challenges that they have faced, the Indian Diaspora continues to make a positive contribution to the economy, and their presence has enriched the local community in numerous ways.

"The Indian Diaspora has made invaluable
contributions to the global community, and
its impact will continue to be felt for
generations to come."

℘

XIII

The Indian Diaspora and Political Participation

The Indian Diaspora has made a significant impact on the political landscape of the countries where they have settled. Through their active participation in the political process, the Indian community abroad has played a vital role in shaping the policies and direction of the local government. In this chapter, we will explore the ways in which the Indian Diaspora has been involved in the political process and the various challenges that they have faced along the way.

One of the most notable ways in which the Indian Diaspora has been involved in the political process is through voting. Many of the Indian immigrants who have settled in other countries are eligible to vote in local elections, and they have used this right to shape the political landscape of their adopted country. Indian immigrants have formed advocacy groups and political organizations to promote their interests and influence the political process, and their participation in the political process has helped to give a voice to the Indian community abroad.

The Indian Diaspora has also made a significant impact on the political landscape through their engagement with political leaders and policymakers. Indian immigrants have used their entrepreneurial spirit and hard work to establish relationships with political leaders and policymakers, and have used these relationships to promote their interests and influence the political process. Additionally, Indian immigrants have used their cultural heritage and values to influence the political landscape, and have helped to promote a more inclusive and diverse society.

However, the Indian Diaspora has also faced various challenges in their political participation. One of the biggest challenges that they have faced is discrimination and prejudice in the political arena. Despite their contributions to the local community and their hard work, many Indian immigrants have faced racism and xenophobia in the political arena, which has made it difficult for them to achieve their political goals. Additionally, many Indian immigrants face language barriers and a lack of access to political information, which has made it difficult for them to fully participate in the political process.

The Indian Diaspora has made a significant impact on the political landscape of the countries where they have settled.

Through their active participation in the political process, their engagement with political leaders and policymakers, and their use of their cultural heritage and values, the Indian community abroad has played a vital role in shaping the policies and direction of the local government. Despite the challenges that they have faced, the Indian Diaspora continues to play an important role in the political arena, and their presence has enriched the local community in numerous ways.

"The Indian Diaspora's efforts to preserve
their cultural identity and heritage serve as a
reminder of the importance of cultural
diversity and pluralism in the world."

৺

XIV

The Indian Diaspora and Preservation of Identity and Culture

Preserving one's cultural identity and heritage is an important aspect of the human experience, and the Indian Diaspora is no exception. Despite facing various challenges, such as adapting to new environments, overcoming language barriers, and maintaining their cultural traditions and values, the Indian community abroad has done an remarkable job of preserving their cultural identity and heritage. In this chapter, we will explore the ways in which the Indian Diaspora has been able to preserve their cultural identity and heritage, as well as the challenges that they have faced along the way.

One of the key ways in which the Indian Diaspora has been able to preserve their cultural identity and heritage is through community engagement and organizations. Many Indian immigrants have formed organizations, such as cultural and religious groups, to connect with their community and maintain their cultural traditions and values. These organizations have provided a platform for the Indian community abroad to celebrate their cultural heritage, share their traditions and values, and support one another through the challenges that they have faced.

Another way in which the Indian Diaspora has been able to preserve their cultural identity and heritage is through the promotion of traditional arts and cultural activities. Many Indian immigrants have been able to preserve their cultural heritage through the promotion of traditional arts and cultural activities, such as music, dance, and theater. Through these activities, the Indian community abroad has been able to maintain their cultural traditions and values and share them with the wider community, enriching the cultural landscape of the countries where they have settled.

However, the Indian Diaspora has also faced various challenges in preserving their cultural identity and heritage. One of the biggest challenges that they have faced is the pressure to conform to the dominant culture and norms of their adopted country. This pressure can lead to the loss of traditional values, cultural practices, and heritage, making it difficult for the Indian community abroad to preserve their cultural identity. Additionally, many Indian immigrants face language barriers and a lack of access to cultural resources, which can make it difficult for them to maintain their cultural traditions and values.

The Indian Diaspora has made a remarkable effort to preserve their cultural identity and heritage despite facing various challenges. Through community engagement and organizations, the promotion of traditional arts and cultural activities, and the determination to maintain their cultural traditions and values, the Indian community abroad has done an outstanding job of preserving their cultural identity and heritage. Their efforts have enriched the cultural landscape of the countries where they have settled, and have provided a unique perspective on Indian culture and heritage to the wider world.

"The Indian Diaspora's success and achievements serve as a testament to the strength and determination of the Indian people, and their unwavering commitment to excellence."

છ

XV

The ongoing Significance and Contributions of the Indian Diaspora

The Indian Diaspora is a global phenomenon that has had a significant impact on Indian culture, society, and the host countries where they have settled. Over the years, the Indian community abroad has made substantial contributions to the cultural, social, and economic development of the countries where they have settled, as well as to the preservation of their cultural identity and heritage. In this chapter, we will summarize the ongoing significance and contributions of the Indian Diaspora.

Firstly, the Indian Diaspora continues to be a major contributor to the cultural, social, and economic development of the host countries where they have settled. The Indian community abroad has played a significant role in promoting Indian culture and heritage in the countries where they have settled, and in enriching the cultural landscape of these countries. Additionally, the Indian Diaspora has made significant contributions to the social and economic development of the countries where they have settled, through their entrepreneurial spirit and their ability to create job opportunities, as well as through their contributions to the fields of science, technology, and medicine.

Secondly, the Indian Diaspora continues to play a critical role in the preservation of their cultural identity and heritage. Despite facing various challenges, such as adapting to new environments, overcoming language barriers, and maintaining their cultural traditions and values, the Indian community abroad has done an outstanding job of preserving their cultural identity and heritage. Through community engagement and organizations, the promotion of traditional arts and cultural activities, and the determination to maintain their cultural traditions and values, the Indian Diaspora has enriched the cultural landscape of the countries where they have settled.

Finally, the ongoing significance and contributions of the Indian Diaspora lie in their ability to bridge the gap between India and the countries where they have settled. The Indian Diaspora serves as a bridge between the two cultures, promoting cultural exchange and understanding, and building a sense of community between the two countries. This bridge has facilitated trade and investment, as well as cultural and social exchange, and has contributed to the overall development of both India and the host countries.

The Indian Diaspora continues to be a significant and ongoing presence in the world, making substantial contributions to the cultural, social, and economic development of the host countries where they have settled, and preserving their cultural identity and heritage. Their contributions have enriched the cultural landscape of the countries where they have settled, and have facilitated cultural and economic exchange between India and the wider world. The Indian Diaspora is a remarkable and ongoing presence that will continue to shape the world for years to come.

"The Indian Diaspora's contributions to the world serve as a reminder of the power of human ingenuity and the limitless potential of the human spirit."

ॐ

Other Books Of The Author

1. The Moments When I Met God
2. Kashiyile Theertha Pathangal
3. GURU GYAN VANI
4. Abhiprerak Gita
5. ASSI SE JAIN GHAT TAK
6. Hopelessness of Arjuna
7. The Soul and It's True Nature
8. Sense of Action (Karma)
9. Action through Wisdom
10. Action through Wisdom
11. THEORY AND PRACTICAL OF EVERY ACTION
12. LOGICAL UNDERSTANDING OF THE SUPREME
13. THE IMPERISHABLE SUPREME
14. Yatra Nishadraj se Hanuman Ghat Tak
15. Yatra Karnatak Ghat se Raja Ghat Tak
16. Yatra Pandey Ghat se Prayagraj Ghat Tak
17. Yatra Ranjendra Prasad Ghat se Dattatreya Ghat Tak
18. YaatraSindhiya Ghat se Gwaliar Ghat Tak
19. Yatra Mangala Gauri Ghat se Hanuman Gadhi Ghat Tak
20. Yatra Gaay Ghat Se Nishad Ghat Tak
21. MAA GANGA, GHATEN EVM UTSAV
22. Ganga Arti Dev Deepavali evam Any Utsav
23. Potentials of Digitalized India
24. VEDIC CONSCIOUSNESS
25. A Brief Introduction to Vedic Science
26. Kashi ke Barah Jyotirling
27. IMPACT OF MOTIVATION
28. Let's have a Milky Way Journey
29. Color Therapy in a Nutshell

59. The Holistic Cow: A Look at the Physical, Spiritual, and Cultural Importance of Cows in India
60. Arts of Healing
61. Exploring the Divine
62. Understanding Five Elements
63. The Etymology of Ram
64. Symbols of India
65. Voice of Change (About Speeches of Great Men)
66. She Speaks (About Speeches of Great Women)
67. Patriotism on Celluloid – Brief About Patriotic Films
68. The Music of Motivation: A Brief Guide to Inspirational Film Songs
69. Unlocking the Secrets of the Dashopanishads
70. A Cultural Mosaic
71. Ancient Traditions, Modern Minds
72. Ecos of Ancient Wisdom
73. Beneath the Surface
74. From Temples to Ashrams
75. Sages of the Subcontinent
76. The Art of Healling (Ayurveda, Yoga & Naturopathy)
77. Indian Kitchen
78. The Festivals of India
79. The Indian Epics Retold
80. The Power of Mantras
81. The Indian River Ganges
82. The Indian Architecture
83. Rites of Passage
84. The Indian Silk Road
85. The Indian Literature
86. The Indian Villages
87. The Indian Folks & Crafts
88. The Way of Buddha
89. The Ramayan of Tulsidas

Contact

DR. JAGADEESH PILLAI

MBA & PhD in Vedic Science

Four Times Guinness World Record Holder

Winner of Mahatma Gandhi Vishwa Shanti Puraskar and
Global Peace Ambassador

Gemology, Astro & Vastu Consultant - Spiritual Counselor

Consultant for designing World Record Ideas

Efficient Tarot Card Reader

9839093003

myrichindia@gmail.com

drjagadeeshpillai@facebook

drjagadeeshpillai@instagram
jagadeeshpillai@youtube

www. JAGADEESHPILLAI.com